D1078986

Dracula

BRAM STOKER

Level 3

Retold by Chris Rice
Series Editors: Andy Hopkins and Jocelyn Potter

Pearson Education Limited

Edinburgh Gate, Harlow,
Essex CM20 2JE, England
and Associated Companies throughout the world.

ISBN 0 582 42663 4

This edition first published 2000

NEW EDITION

Typeset by Pantek Arts, Maidstone, Kent
Set in 11/14pt Bembo
Printed in Denmark by Norhaven A/S, Viborg

Published by Pearson Education Limited in association with
Penguin Books Ltd, both companies being subsidiaries of Pearson Plc

Acknowledgements:
Photographs © BBC 1977

For a complete list of the titles available in the Penguin Readers series please write to your local
Pearson Education office or to: Marketing Department, Penguin Longman Publishing,
5 Bentinck Street, London W1M 5RN.

Contents

Introduction

There, on a bed of earth, was Count Dracula. At first Jonathan thought he was dead. His eyes were open, and his face was pale. No breath came from his mouth or nose, and there was no sign of a heart in his chest. But there was something about his eyes that frightened Jonathan. They did not have the glassy look of death. They looked up into the air above him, but they were filled with a terrible hate.

Count Dracula lives in a large castle in Transylvania, but he wants to buy a house in England. A London law company sends Jonathan Harker to Castle Dracula to help the count with his business. Dracula is friendly and polite to his guest, but something is wrong. Why are the doors to the rooms in the castle all locked? Why aren't there any mirrors? Why does the count only wake up at night, and why does he seem so strangely interested in pictures of Jonathan's girlfriend, Mina? When Jonathan discovers a terrible secret about Count Dracula, he wants to escape. But how? He is a prisoner in the castle. Will he ever see England and Mina again?

When does a man stop being a man? When does he start to become something different? Towards the end of the 1800s, many writers became interested in questions like these. Two of the most successful stories on this subject were Robert Louis Stevenson's *Dr Jekyll and Mr Hyde* (1886), and Oscar Wilde's *Picture of Dorian Gray* (1891). Then, in June 1897, came Bram Stoker's *Dracula*.

Stoker's mother, writing to him in London from Ireland, said: 'No book since Mrs Shelley's *Frankenstein* has been better or more frightening than yours. *Dracula* will make you a lot of money, and you will be famous.' *Dracula* became a bestseller and

Stoker made some money. But he did not become famous until after his death. *Dracula* is now one of the most famous names in fiction. You can find the book in more than forty languages, and there have been more films about Count Dracula than about any other fictional person except Sherlock Holmes. Visitors to Romania are now shown 'Dracula's Castle' (but Bram Stoker never visited the country).

Dracula was not the first story about vampires. Byron wrote about them (*The Giaour* 1813) and John Polidori wrote *The Vampyre* in 1818 (one year before Mary Shelley wrote *Frankenstein*). Heinrich Marschner's *Der Vampyr* was popular in Germany a long time before Stoker wrote *Dracula*.

Vampire stories are very old. People in Slavonic countries have believed for hundreds of years that vampires exist. In these stories, bad people became vampires after they died. They returned as large bats and drank the blood of sleeping people. These people then became vampires, too. If vampires were able to find blood, they never died. People believed that they could protect themselves from vampires with plants, like garlic, and with fire.

When religion came to the Slavs, stories about vampires did not stop. But people believed that some religious things, like holy bread and the cross, could also protect them from vampires. There was only one way to kill a vampire – and to save the soul of the dead person. That, they believed, was with a thick, sharp piece of wood through the heart.

Abraham Stoker was born in Dublin, Ireland, in 1847. He was an excellent student at university (Trinity College), and he was also a very good runner and footballer. While he was a student, Stoker went to a Dublin theatre and saw the great English actor, Henry Irving. Stoker fell in love with the theatre, and he never forgot Henry Irving.

After university, he worked in Irish government offices. It was a boring life for him, but he made it more interesting; he gave talks at the university about English writers and votes for women. He also wrote about the theatre for Dublin newspapers, and his first story, *The Chain of Destiny*, was printed in the *Shamrock* magazine in 1875.

In 1878 he got married, left his job in Ireland and moved to London. There, he found work with the actor that he first saw in Dublin eleven years before. He became the personal secretary to Sir Henry Irving. Irving was the most famous actor and producer in the English theatre at that time. His favourite plays were by Shakespeare, but he also enjoyed producing and acting in a different kind of play. These stories were more exciting and frightening than real life, and perhaps Stoker first became interested in vampires from these plays. Perhaps, too, Stoker was thinking of Henry Irving when he wrote about Count Dracula. Many people believe that.

Stoker travelled around Britain and to the USA many times with Irving and his theatre company. During this time, he started writing seriously. His first book, in 1879, was about the law courts in Ireland. After that, he wrote fifteen fictional books. A book of children's stories, *Under the Sunset* (1881), was his first. *Dracula* (1897) is his most famous.

In 1905 Henry Irving died and Stoker wrote two books about him – *Personal Reminiscences of Henry Irving* – the following year.

Bram Stoker died in London in 1912.

Chapter 1   Castle Dracula

As the carriage moved quickly along the rough, dry road, Jonathan Harker looked out at the changing view. Behind him was a land of small, green hills and colourful fields of fruit trees. Now he was driving into the Transylvanian mountains through a thick forest. It was getting dark, and the other people in the carriage were quiet and afraid. A woman opposite him reached towards him and put something in his hand. It was a small, silver cross. 'Wear it around your neck,' she said. 'You'll be safe.'

Suddenly the driver stopped the carriage. 'You get out here,' he called to Jonathan.

Nervously, Jonathan got out. He watched as the carriage drove away. Then another big black carriage came out of the trees. The driver helped Jonathan in and drove up into the forest. Jonathan looked out into the night. He saw dark shapes with bright red eyes following the carriage through the trees. They were wolves.

The hours passed and it began to snow. Suddenly Jonathan looked up through the trees. There was a large, black castle on top of a mountain.

'Castle Dracula, at last,' he thought.

Soon he was standing in front of a big, old wooden door. The carriage drove away. Jonathan stood in the cold and waited, listening nervously to the wolves outside the castle walls. Then he heard a noise from the other side of the door. It opened. A tall man dressed in black stood there.

'My house is your house,' he smiled. 'Come freely and go safely. Leave here a little of the happiness that you bring.'

'Count★ Dracula?' asked Jonathan.

★Count: An old European title that was given by the king to men from important families.

'I am Dracula. I am glad, Mr Harker, to have you in my house. I will carry your bags – it is late, and my servants are asleep.'

Jonathan followed him up the stairs into a large, well-lit dining room. The room was warmed by a big wood fire. A hot meal was waiting for him on the table.

'Forgive me if I do not eat with you,' the count said, as Jonathan sat down. 'I have already eaten.'

After dinner Jonathan sat opposite the count by the fire.

'Your boss at the law company, Mr Hawkins, says many good things about you,' the count said. 'I am very pleased that you are here as my guest. I am not often able to practise my English.'

The count talked about his plans to move to England. Jonathan studied his face. It was an unusual face: very pale and mysterious with a long, well-shaped nose, cold, red eyes and a thin mouth filled with pointed, white teeth. Looking down, Jonathan noticed his long, sharp fingernails. There was hair on both sides of his hands.

Silence fell at last, but Jonathan could still hear the frightening sound of wolves outside the castle. The count moved his face towards Jonathan's.

'My children are excited tonight,' he smiled. 'We have so few visitors.'

Jonathan smiled politely, but he felt sick at the smell of Dracula's breath. 'The smell of death,' he thought.

'Come,' Dracula said, standing up. 'It is getting light. You are tired after your long journey, and I have talked too much. Forgive me. I will show you to your room.'

◆

Jonathan slept late the next morning. He found breakfast ready for him in the dining room. There was no sign of the count, so Jonathan then decided to look around the castle. Many doors were locked, but one was open. Inside there was a large library. Jonathan was surprised that there were English books on the shelves and English newspapers on the desks. He spent the rest of the day there, reading happily.

In the late afternoon the count walked in.

'I am glad that you have found your way here,' he said. 'Since I decided to buy a house in England, I have tried to learn something about English life. I am sorry that I only know the language from books. I hope to talk to you, Mr Harker, and to learn it better. And now, our business.'

Dracula sat down opposite Jonathan and continued: 'Tell me about the house that your company has bought for me in England. There will be some papers that I must put my name to. Of course, I would like to know everything.'

'The house is called Carfax,' Jonathan began to explain. 'It's to the north of London. It has a lot of land. Most of the land is covered with trees, so it's quite dark. The house is large and old, with few windows. Next to it, there's an old, empty church. That also belongs to the house. I'm afraid that you will find Carfax a lonely house. Your only neighbour is a doctor who looks after a hospital for mad people.'

'I am glad that the house is old,' replied the count. 'I come from an old family and I do not like to live in a house without history. And the darkness does not worry me. I am an old man, and I often think about death. I do not fear darkness.'

He wrote his name on the papers and walked out of the room. Jonathan followed him into the dining room. Dinner was waiting, but again the count did not eat. 'I went out to eat today,' he told Jonathan. 'I am not hungry.'

That evening and the following ones passed in the same way as the first. Then one day, about a week after he arrived, a strange thing happened. Jonathan was standing by his window. He was shaving in front of a little mirror from his travelling bag.

Suddenly he heard a quiet voice in his ear say: 'Good morning.' Jonathan jumped with fear and cut himself on the neck. The count was standing next to him. Jonathan looked in the mirror again, but he could only see himself.

'Why can't I see him in the mirror?' he thought.

He turned again, and saw a strange, hungry look in Dracula's eyes. The count was watching the small stream of blood coming out of the cut on Jonathan's neck.

Without thinking, Jonathan lifted his hand to the blood. As he did that, he touched the little silver cross around his neck. The count's face changed. His eyes shone red and he began to shake. Then, without a word, he picked up the mirror and threw it out of the window. There was a long silence, then Jonathan heard the crash of broken glass on the rocks far below. The count turned angrily:

'I will not have mirrors in my house,' he shouted. Then, seconds later, he said more softly: 'Try not to cut yourself. It is more dangerous in this country than you think.'

When the count left the room, Jonathan looked out of the window at his broken mirror. The ground was a long way down. For the first time he realized that he wanted to leave. He wanted to go home. 'But will he give me permission to leave?' he thought. 'Am I really his guest? Or am I, perhaps, his prisoner?'

Chapter 2   Three Women

The days and nights passed in the same way. Jonathan got up late, had breakfast and read in the library. At night he sat by the fireside. He listened with interest as the count talked with great feeling about the history of his family and of his country. This was almost the same thing, because the Dracula family seemed to be at the centre of all Transylvania's history.

'It is more dangerous in this country than you think.'

Sometimes the count talked about more ordinary things: about England, law, ships and trains. Jonathan was surprised that Dracula knew so much. He wanted to send things to England, to a town by the sea. But which town?

'Why not Whitby?' Jonathan suggested. 'My girlfriend Mina, and her best friend Lucy, are going on holiday there. It's a fine old fishing town in the north of England.'

The count was interested. Whitby seemed a good idea. He also wanted to hear more about Mina. 'She's the girl that I'm going to marry,' Jonathan said, showing the count a photograph. 'And this,' he said, pointing to the other girl in the picture, 'is Lucy, her best friend.' The count studied the photograph and smiled.

'They are pretty girls,' he said. 'Your Miss Mina – she will want to know how you are. Have you written to her since you arrived?'

'I have not had much time to send any letters,' Jonathan replied.

'Then write now, my good friend. But first I want you to write to Mr Hawkins. Tell him that you will stay with me for another month.'

Jonathan's blood ran suddenly cold. 'Do you want me to stay for so long?' he asked weakly.

'Yes, I do. Your job here is to look after my business, and my business makes a longer visit necessary. Now,' he said, handing Jonathan envelopes and paper, 'please write only about business in your letters. And you can say that you are well, of course.'

Jonathan went to the desk and wrote two short letters. The count took them. Before he went, he said: 'I must tell you something, my young friend. If you go into any other part of the castle, do not fall asleep there. The castle is old. Strange things have happened here, and bad dreams will come to you. In these rooms, and in your bedroom, you are safe.'

◆

Later that night, Jonathan went down to the great door at the front of the castle. It was locked, as usual. 'The key's probably in the count's room,' he thought. He walked round the castle and found one or two open rooms, but they went nowhere. Then he noticed a door at the end of a short passage. At first he thought it was locked. But he lifted and pushed it, and he was then able to open it. Feeling his way up some dark stairs, he found himself in a pleasant moonlit room. It seemed to be next to his own bedroom.

Jonathan put his head out of the window and enjoyed the night air. Then he noticed a movement at a window below, and he could not believe his eyes. 'This is impossible,' he thought. 'I'm dreaming.' He watched, frozen with fear. Dracula climbed out of the window, and moved down the wall like some terrible animal of the night. His fingers and toes used every little space between the stones, and his black clothes flew up around him in the wind. Then he disappeared into the shadows at the bottom of the castle wall.

Jonathan could not think or act. He felt weak and afraid. There was a bed on the other side of the room opposite the window. 'I'll lie down here for a short time,' he thought, 'until I feel stronger.'

He closed his eyes and began to feel sleepy. But, after a short time, he had a strange feeling that he was not alone.

Three young women were watching him from the shadows, and they were talking in low voices. They moved out into the moonlight. He saw then, through half-open eyes, that they were very beautiful. When they laughed, the moonlight shone on long, white teeth.

As they came nearer, their eyes shone red. They filled the air with their excited laughing. Jonathan felt in his heart that they were evil. But for some reason he did not feel afraid. There was something about them that excited him. He wanted them to come to him, to touch him ...

Three young women were watching him from the shadows.

The fairest girl went down on her knees next to the bed and put her face close to his. Jonathan felt her soft breath on the side of his neck. Two sharp teeth were resting lightly on his skin. He closed his eyes and waited. He was unable to move . . .

Suddenly there was a loud noise. He opened his eyes and saw, by the side of his bed, a tall, black shape. It was the count. His face was as white as death but his eyes burned like two small fires.

'I told you not to touch him!' the count said angrily. He took the woman by her neck and threw her across the room. 'This man is mine! I will use him first. Then, and only then . . .'

'So, what fun can we have tonight?' one of the women asked.

There was a bag at Dracula's feet. Something was moving inside it. Dracula kicked it across the floor towards the women, and Jonathan felt sick. The sound inside the bag was the frightened cry of a baby. The women pulled at the bag like hungry animals. The baby's cries grew louder, then suddenly stopped. The room filled with a strange, green mist, and Jonathan fell into a deep, dreamless sleep.

Chapter 3   A Bag of Blood

That evening the count said nothing about the night before. He just brought out more writing paper and asked Jonathan to write Mina three letters. 'In the first one, say that you have almost finished your work. Say that you are going to leave in a few days,' the count ordered him. 'In the second letter, say that you are leaving the next morning. In the third, say that you have left the castle. You have arrived in Bistritz.'

When Jonathan gave him a worried look, he explained:

'The post is slow in this part of the country. I do not want your friends to think that something has happened to you. I will post these letters at the right time. Then they will know when you are going to arrive home.'

Jonathan wrote the three letters. 'I cannot refuse,' he told himself. 'I have to follow his orders. I'm his prisoner here, and my life is in danger.'

◆

The next morning, Jonathan woke to the sound of voices — ordinary voices. Running to the dining-room window, he looked down. Some men were taking long wooden boxes off a cart.

'Free men!' Jonathan thought excitedly. 'If I can write a letter quickly, they can take it to the outside world.'

He ran to his room for the paper that he kept in his bag. But where was his bag with his ticket and his money? Where was the suit that he travelled in, and his coat? They were not there!

When he returned to the window, he could not see the men or the cart. For the rest of the day, Jonathan could hear them at work somewhere below in the castle. Something was happening.

That evening he sat by his window and waited. Soon after dark, he saw movement at Dracula's window.

Dracula climbed out and moved down the wall in the same way as the night before. But this time he was wearing Jonathan's clothes.

Everything now became clear. 'He's going to show himself in Bistritz and post the letters,' Jonathan thought. 'The people will believe that he is me. They'll think that I'm already on my way home. Nobody will know that I'm still in the castle. Dracula will be able to do what he likes with me. I must escape. I have to get the key of the door. I have to get into the count's room. But how? His room is always locked.'

Then Jonathan thought of a plan. 'I know his window,' he thought. 'I've seen him climb out of it. It's lower than mine, to the left. The stones in the castle wall are big and rough. The spaces between them are big. If I take off my boots, perhaps I can climb down the wall into his room. It's dangerous, I know, but what can I do?'

◆

Jonathan waited until the morning. The night was too dangerous. He knew that Dracula slept during the day. He took off his boots, climbed out of his window and moved slowly and carefully down and across the castle wall. He did not look down. Finally he arrived at the count's window, and climbed into his room.

'Is this really the count's room?' he asked himself. It was empty except for some old money on the dirty floor. And there weren't any keys. But behind a door in the corner of the room, Jonathan found something interesting: some stone steps.

He nervously started to go down them, and he noticed a strange, earthy smell. It was the smell of Dracula's breath. The smell became stronger and more unpleasant as he went down. Finally, at the bottom, there was a dark passage. He followed it, and came into a room with an earth floor. At the far end, Jonathan could see the boxes that were brought by the men with the cart. There were about fifty of them, and they were all now filled with earth. Near them was another, older box. Jonathan walked across and looked inside. He stepped back with a cry.

There, on a bed of earth, was Count Dracula. At first Jonathan thought he was dead. His eyes were open, and his face was pale. No breath came from his mouth or nose, and there was no sign of a heart in his chest. But there was something about his eyes that frightened Jonathan. They did not have the glassy look of death. They looked up into the air above him, but they were filled with a terrible hate. Jonathan wanted to find the key, but he could not touch the count. He was too afraid. He left as quickly as he could. Then he returned to his own room.

That night the count came to Jonathan's room at his usual time.

'Tonight, my friend, we must say goodbye. Tomorrow you return to your own country, and I, too, have to make a journey. In the morning my carriage will take you to the Bistritz road, and you will be in Bistritz by tomorrow evening. I hope I shall see you again at Castle Dracula.'

'Why can't I go tonight?' asked Jonathan.

'Because, my dear sir, my carriage is busy.'

'But I can walk. I want to go now.'

'And your bags?'

'They're not important. I can send for them later.'

The count smiled. 'All right! You do not have to stay if you are ready to leave. But I am sad that you want to go so quickly.'

Jonathan followed the count down the stairs to the great door. The count stopped, lifted his hand and said: 'Listen!'

From the other side of the door came the sound of wolves in the forest. Dracula unlocked the door and opened it. The sound of wolves immediately became louder. Jonathan looked through the door and saw wolves jumping up and down. Their hungry red mouths were wide open.

'Shut the door! I'll wait until morning,' cried Jonathan at last. He turned away because he did not want Dracula to see his tears. The door closed with a crash, and the sound of the wolves became quieter.

◆

The next day, in the early morning, Jonathan decided to go back to the count's room. He felt braver now. 'The count's going to kill me tonight if I stay,' he told himself. 'If I fall off the wall this morning, that's a better way to die.'

He ran to the window. Then he climbed down and across the wall and into the count's room. He went through the door in the corner of the room, down the steps and along the dark passage to the room with the earth floor.

He walked straight to Dracula's box and lifted the top. When he looked inside, his heart almost stopped. Dracula was there, inside the box, but he looked different. His face was fatter than usual, and his skin was not white – it was the colour of red wine. Blood ran from the corners of his mouth, down his neck and on to his clothes. He smelled of blood. And on his face was the look of a wild animal that has killed. Then it has fed until it cannot feed again.

Jonathan could not leave now. He had to try to find the key. He searched in Dracula's pockets, but they were empty. For the first time in his life, Jonathan wanted to kill. He wanted to destroy this hateful bag of blood lying in its box. He picked up a heavy stone, lifted it above Dracula's head and dropped it. But, as the stone left Jonathan's hands, Dracula opened his eyes. For a second, the stone seemed to hang in the air. Then it fell slowly. It touched the side of Dracula's face softly, without hurting him. Jonathan could not move. Dracula's eyes were turning towards him and he was slowly beginning to smile . . .

Seconds later, Jonathan turned and ran. Filled with an animal fear, he wanted to leave the boxes, the evil smell and the count's terrible bloodthirsty smile behind him. He wanted to be as far away from them as possible. He hurried up the stairs, out of the window and up the castle wall as quickly as he could. Back in his room, he threw himself on to his bed and waited. 'He's going to kill me now,' he thought. He couldn't shake the picture of Dracula's terrible smile out of his mind. 'I know it. I have no hope. In a short time I'll be dead. He'll drink my blood, and then he'll go to England for fresh blood. What can I do?'

He lay on his bed, shaking with fear. He waited. But, to his surprise, nothing happened. A few hours later he heard the sound of horses and of men singing. He left his bed, crossed the room and looked down from his window. There was a cart filled with wooden boxes. Inside one of them, Jonathan knew, was Dracula. He was on his way to England.

Dracula was there, inside the box.

For a minute Jonathan stopped feeling afraid. But then he remembered that there was still one problem. 'Tomorrow morning I can leave,' he thought. 'But what will happen tonight? Dracula's away, so who will protect me from those three terrible women? They want my blood ...' He remembered Dracula's words to them: *'I will use him first. Then, and only then ...'*

Jonathan went to his door and listened. At first there was silence. But then he heard something in the passage just outside his door. The sound of dresses, the sound of women laughing ... Jonathan's fear returned. He went down on his knees, held his hands together and lifted his eyes to the sky. 'Please help me, someone,' he cried. 'Will I ever see England and Mina again?'

Chapter 4   Mina and Lucy

Mina Murray was a pretty girl, but her friend, Lucy Westenra, was very beautiful. Many men fell in love with Lucy. The three that she liked best were Jack Seward and his friends, Quincey Morris and Arthur Holmwood. Jack Seward was a doctor, and he looked after a hospital for mad people north of London. Quincey Morris was an American adventurer. Arthur Holmwood came from a famous, old English family.

In August the two girls went to Whitby for a holiday together. Lucy talked excitedly about the three men in her life. She couldn't decide which man she wanted to marry.

One day Mina was reading a letter in the garden when she heard Lucy's excited voice. She looked up as Lucy ran towards her.

'I've decided!' Lucy laughed. 'I'm going to marry Arthur.'

'Oh Lucy, I'm so happy for you,' Mina said.

But Lucy noticed something sad in her friend's voice and said: 'What's the matter, Mina?'

Mina showed her the letter in her hand. 'It's Jonathan. I'm worried about him. This is only the third letter from him in more than a month. His letters are so short and cold. There's something wrong. I know there is.'

Lucy read the letter, then held Mina in her arms. 'Oh Mina,' she said. 'Don't worry. I'm sure there's a simple explanation.'

That night there was a terrible storm. It was the worst storm in Whitby in people's memory. There were thick black clouds, strong winds and heavy rain. But the strangest thing was a thick mist that came in from the sea. In the middle of the storm, out of the mist, sailed a mysterious, foreign ship, *The Demeter*. The ship was empty except for one man. He was dead and he was tied to the wheel. As the ship reached land, a large black dog jumped off. It ran across the beach and disappeared in the narrow streets of the old town.

Two nights later, Mina woke up with a strange feeling. Lucy was not in the room. Mina ran out of the house. It was dark, but suddenly the moon came from behind a cloud. Her friend was half-sitting, half-lying on their favourite seat in the garden. A tall black shape was standing next to her.

Mina cried out and ran towards her friend. When she reached her, Lucy was completely alone. She was still in the same position, with her head over the back of the seat. Mina took her by the hand and helped her back to the house. When they were inside, Mina noticed two little red wounds on Lucy's neck.

The next night, Mina locked the bedroom door and took the key to bed with her. Twice Lucy got up in her sleep and tried to open the door and windows. Mina took her back to bed, and then looked out of the window. She saw nothing – only a full moon and a large bat flying in circles above the garden.

In the next few days, Lucy ate, slept and had plenty of fresh air, but she grew paler and weaker. Twice Mina found her during the night, lying with her head out of the open window. The wounds in her neck were growing larger.

One morning a letter came for Mina. It was from a nurse at a hospital in Budapest. Jonathan Harker was in the hospital. He was very ill. 'When he arrived here,' the nurse wrote, 'he talked wildly about wolves, blood and vampires. We do not know how he came here. But something evil has happened to him.'

'Oh Lucy!' Mina said, holding her friend tightly. 'He's safe, but I must go to him.'

◆

One of the madmen in Jack Seward's hospital was acting very strangely. Again and again he repeated, 'He's near!' Then one night he escaped. Dr Seward and his men caught Renfield, the madman, outside a church near Carfax House. While they were carrying him back to the hospital, Renfield kicked wildly. He screamed at a bat that was flying in and out of the trees.

One day Arthur Holmwood came to see Dr Seward. He asked the doctor to visit Lucy. She was staying at her mother's house in Hillingdon, not far from Dr Seward's hospital.

'Lucy's so weak,' Arthur said. 'She lies down all the time. She's getting worse every day.'

Dr Seward went immediately. Lucy was pale and weak, but he could find no reason for her illness – except for two ugly red wounds on her neck. He sent some blood to London for a check, and a report came back. Nothing was wrong with it.

'I don't understand it,' Dr Seward told Arthur. 'I'm going to ask my old friend and university teacher to see her. Professor Van Helsing, of Amsterdam, knows everything about unusual illnesses like this.'

Chapter 5   Professor Van Helsing

Professor Abraham Van Helsing arrived in Hillingdon three days later. He looked at Lucy for a few minutes, then he went back to Amsterdam. The next day Lucy seemed better.

Again and again he repeated, 'He's near!'

But if Lucy seemed better, Renfield did not. He was very quiet after his escape. He just sat in a corner without speaking. Dr Seward tried to start conversations with him, but Renfield always answered in the same way: 'He's left me. There's no hope. He's left me.'

◆

On the third day after Van Helsing's visit, Lucy became ill again. Dr Seward immediately asked Van Helsing to return.

The professor arrived the following evening, and Dr Seward took him up to Lucy's room. Lucy was worse than before. She was very pale and weak. As Van Helsing looked at her, excited voices from the doorway broke the silence. It was Arthur Holmwood and Quincey Morris.

'I came as soon as I could,' said Arthur. 'She's worse, I hear.'

Van Helsing took the two men outside and said: 'She is in the greatest danger.'

'Danger?' cried Arthur. 'But what can we do? I will give the blood from my body to save her.'

'Good,' Van Helsing replied. 'That is exactly what she needs. She has lost most of the blood from her body, and she needs the blood of a young and healthy man like you. Please, Mr Holmwood, take off your coat. We must act immediately.'

Without a word, Arthur took off his coat and pulled up the arm of his shirt. Lucy didn't feel the cut that was made in her arm. She was too ill. Ten minutes later, the blood from Arthur's arm began to give colour to her pale face again, and her breaths became easier.

'We will now leave Miss Lucy. She must sleep,' Van Helsing said. 'Tomorrow I shall return. But we have to do one more thing before we leave.'

He went downstairs and returned with a box. He put it on Lucy's bed. 'Open it,' he said, with a smile. Lucy put her hand in the box and pulled out some little white flowers.

'Oh!' she said. 'These are garlic flowers. Is this a joke, Professor?'

Van Helsing looked at her seriously, rested his hand on hers and said: 'This is no joke. Please take them, or you will be in great danger.' He saw that she was frightened. So he continued in a softer voice: 'Do not be afraid. I am here to help you. These flowers look ordinary, but they can protect you. Believe me.'

Van Helsing stood up. While the others watched with surprise, he shut the windows. Then he took a handful of the flowers and pressed them all round the windows, the door and the fireplace. Finally, he made a small ring with the other flowers and placed it around Lucy's neck.

'Do not open the windows or the door tonight,' he told her before he left. 'And do not take these flowers from your neck. It is very, very important.'

◆

The next day, at eight o'clock, Van Helsing and Dr Seward went together to the Westenra house. They were met by Lucy's mother.

'Lucy seems better,' she said. 'I've just looked into her room. She was sleeping well, so I didn't wake her up.'

'Good,' said the professor. 'So my idea was successful.'

'Perhaps *my* idea was successful too,' Mrs Westenra smiled. 'I went into her room before I went to bed last night. She was sleeping quietly, but there was no air in the room, and there was a strong smell from some terrible flowers round her neck. I took them away and opened the windows. You'll be pleased with her, I'm sure.'

Van Helsing's face went pale. He said nothing, because he knew about Mrs Westenra's weak heart. It was dangerous to frighten her. But when she left the room, he ran up the stairs to Lucy.

'This is bad news,' Van Helsing said to Seward, carefully studying Lucy's pale face. 'I have to return to Amsterdam today, but you must sleep in this house every night. In this room, if necessary. Boxes of fresh flowers will arrive every day. You must do exactly what I did last night. I shall return in four days, or before, if you need me. Guard her well.'

'Guard her?' Dr Seward asked himself, as Van Helsing left the room. 'Guard her against what?'

Chapter 6   Only the Beginning

The next few days were hard for Jack Seward. He was at the hospital all day, and at Hillingdon by night. Every morning a fresh box of garlic flowers arrived by special post from Holland. Seward did exactly as the professor showed him on the first night. He did not like it, because it seemed too unscientific. Dr Seward was a very scientific man. But it seemed to succeed. The colour slowly returned to Lucy's face, and the wounds in her neck began to get better.

But he was very tired at night. He was woken up many times by strange sounds from outside Lucy's window. At first he thought that a tree was moving against the glass in the wind. But the next day he realized that there was no tree near the window. 'It was probably my imagination,' he told himself.

◆

Renfield was also making trouble. One day he suddenly attacked two men. He was walking in the garden with a guard when he noticed some men. They were driving a cart along the road from Carfax. The guard was just able to pull Renfield away. Dr Seward decided to take the men's names and to give them some money.

Early one evening, Seward was sitting in his office. He was reading the newspaper before he went over to Hillingdon. Tired from writing reports, he was falling asleep over a story about an escaped wolf. In his dreams the wolf was jumping in through the window – when suddenly, the door crashed open. It was Renfield. He ran straight at Seward with a kitchen knife. Seward stood up and tried to keep the table between them, but Renfield was too quick. He pushed the knife into Seward's left arm. Angrily, Seward hit Renfield on the head with a heavy book from his desk.

Renfield dropped the knife and fell, face down, on to the floor. Blood from the wound in Seward's arm fell on to the floor next to Renfield's face. The guards came into the room and lifted Renfield to his feet. He kicked wildly as they took him from the room. He screamed, 'Blood is life!'

But Seward wasn't listening. He only had eyes for Renfield's screaming mouth. 'I don't believe it,' Seward thought. 'The madman's mouth is red. He drank my blood as it fell to the floor. The man's sicker than I thought.'

'Blood is life!' Renfield screamed again, as they carried him from the room. And Seward, weak with pain and lost blood, fell to the floor.

◆

Seward sat up in bed, feeling very weak. 'Perhaps I've lost too much blood,' he thought. He looked at his watch. It was ten o'clock – and he wasn't at Hillingdon with Lucy!

'Hillingdon? Impossible, my dear Seward,' said Dr Hennessey, one of his assistants. 'You must stay in bed.'

'I'll stay here if you visit the Westenra house,' Dr Seward said. 'Tell Miss Lucy to do the usual things,' he added, as Hennessey was leaving. 'She'll understand.'

Seward slept late the next morning. He was woken up by a boy with a special message from Amsterdam. Seward opened it and read:

Be at Hillingdon tonight! Very important.
Arriving early on 19th. Van Helsing.

23

'Oh no!' Seward thought. 'That was last night. What does Van Helsing mean?'

◆

He did not wait for breakfast – he drove straight to Hillingdon. It was still early. He did not want to wake Lucy or her mother, so he rang quietly. He hoped to bring a servant to the door. No answer. He rang again. Still no answer. He put his ear to the letter box. Everything was silent. He thought that something was wrong.

He walked round the house, looking for an open window. Everything was carefully shut and locked. But then he came to Lucy's mother's room on the ground floor. Her window was broken and there was blood on the glass. In the flower bed below the window there were signs of an animal's feet. 'Perhaps they were made by a dog,' Seward thought. 'Or even . . .' He remembered the escaped wolf, and shook his head. 'No, that's not possible,' he told himself, feeling stupid. He stood up and looked around him.

The house and garden were unnaturally quiet. He went down on his knees and looked at the signs in the earth more carefully. Suddenly he heard a sound on the path behind him. He jumped up, ready to defend himself. But it was only Van Helsing. In a few breathless words, he told the professor about Renfield and the message from Holland.

'I am afraid we are too late,' Van Helsing said. He put his hand through the broken window and opened it. They climbed into Lucy's mother's bedroom.

There, on the bed, lay Lucy and her mother. Great fear showed on Mrs Westenra's face. Seward felt her hand. She was dead. Her other hand was holding tightly on to a ring of flowers. Seconds before dying, she probably reached out for her daughter. Then she pulled the flowers from Lucy's neck.

Lucy lay by her side. The wounds on her neck were wide open, and there were the signs of new bites. Van Helsing held her hand and placed his ear close to her chest.

'It's not too late!' he cried at last. 'Quickly! Get some hot water and towels. We must keep her warm!'

When Dr Seward ran through the dining room, he found all the servants on the floor. He smelled their breath. 'Something in their drink,' he thought. 'Something sent them to sleep.' Returning with a bowl of hot water and some towels, he told the professor about the servants.

'Go and wake them,' Van Helsing said impatiently. 'We need their help. And get Mr Holmwood. It is possible that Miss Lucy will die. He will want to be here.'

Because Lucy was so weak, Van Helsing did not want to wake her. He thought it was unwise to give her fresh blood. Dr Seward watched her while she slept. Short, painful breaths escaped from her open mouth. Then he looked more carefully. There was something strange about her mouth. Her teeth seemed longer and sharper than usual. But minutes later, she opened her eyes and the colour returned to her face. She was, again, the beautiful young girl he loved.

Arthur was brave. He sat with Lucy all the time, and his face never showed the sadness in his heart. Van Helsing later sent him to sleep in the sitting room. Seward stayed by Lucy's bed.

◆

At about six o'clock in the morning, Van Helsing came in and gave Seward a rest. He looked at Lucy's neck. As he looked, a strange, cold feeling passed over him. The skin on her neck was smooth and unbroken.

'Look,' he said to Seward. 'The two red wounds have completely disappeared.' Then, looking sadly up at Seward, he

Dr Seward watched her while she slept.

said: 'She is dying. It will not be long now. Wake that young man. He must be with her at the end.'

When Arthur came, Lucy opened her eyes. 'Arthur, my love,' she said, in a low voice.

Arthur moved to kiss her. But Van Helsing stopped him: 'No, not yet. Just hold her hand.' Lucy's eyes closed, and she seemed to sleep. Dr Seward noticed again the strange changes to her face: the tight skin, the open mouth and the long, sharp teeth.

Then, in a soft, sleepy voice, Lucy spoke again: 'Arthur, kiss me.' As Arthur moved towards her, she opened her eyes. They were as hard as stone. Before Arthur could kiss her, Van Helsing roughly pulled him back.

'Not for your life!' he shouted. 'Not for your living soul!'

An angry shadow passed across Lucy's face, and her sharp teeth closed with a terrible metallic sound. Then a cloud of calmness came over her, and she was suddenly a pale, tired, dying girl. She tried to smile, but she was too weak.

Van Helsing looked at Arthur. 'Now, my boy. Take her hand in yours and kiss her now. But not on the mouth. And only once.' Arthur kissed her, and Lucy's eyes closed. Her breaths became more difficult, and then they stopped.

'It's finished,' said Dr Seward.

'No,' Van Helsing replied. 'I am afraid that this is only the beginning.'

Chapter 7   Beautiful but Evil

A few days later, the newspapers began to report attacks on young children in north London. The children disappeared, but they were found later – after midnight. They looked weak and pale, and they had wounds in their necks.

Van Helsing read the reports. 'What do you think?' he asked the doctor.

'Lucy had neck wounds too,' Seward replied.

'Exactly.'

'You don't mean . . .' Seward began.

Van Helsing continued: 'Have you still no idea how Lucy died? She lost too much blood. How? Through wounds in her neck, like these children. Now tell me – you were always a quick student. What made those wounds?'

'I've heard of vampire bats in South America that drink blood,' Seward said slowly. 'But we don't have bats like those here in England. You want me to say that a vampire made these wounds. A vampire that is also a living person. Only a madman can believe that.'

Van Helsing felt sorry for the young doctor. 'There is something worse – I have to say it. It was a different vampire that drank these children's blood. It is not the same as the vampire that drank Lucy's blood. Lucy was the vampire that attacked the children.'

Jack Seward looked angrily at his old friend, but Van Helsing continued: 'It is true. Of course, it is hard for you to believe. But I can prove it.'

He took Seward first to the hospital. There they looked at the wounds on the neck of one of the children. They were exactly like the wounds on Lucy's neck. Then the two doctors went to the tomb where Lucy's coffin lay.

'What are you going to do?' Seward wanted to know.

Van Helsing opened the top of the coffin and told Seward to look inside. Seward looked. It was empty.

'Now,' Van Helsing said, 'we must wait outside the tomb.'

◆

They waited until after midnight. Then they saw something in the darkness – a white shape was moving through the trees. Van Helsing stepped out from behind a tree. The shape suddenly disappeared, leaving a small child asleep on the ground.

They took the child to a place where a policeman could easily find it. Then they waited until daylight before Van Helsing took Dr Seward back to the tomb. Lucy was lying in her coffin. She was not pale like an ordinary dead body. The colour in her face made her more beautiful than ever.

Van Helsing opened her mouth and showed Seward her teeth.

'See – they are like knife points now. How many times does she have to use them on a child's neck before you believe me?'

Seward could not take his eyes off the evil but beautiful face of the woman that he loved. 'What do we have to do?' he asked in a low, flat voice.

'Cut off her head, fill her mouth with garlic and push a thick piece of wood through her heart. But not now. We are not ready. And I must ask Arthur Holmwood for his permission.'

Chapter 8   To Save a Soul

Later the same day, Arthur Holmwood and his best friend, Quincey Morris, visited Van Helsing at the hospital. Of course, Arthur was angry with Van Helsing. He was very unhappy about Lucy's death. The idea of cutting her head off made him sick. He refused to listen at first, but Quincey said: 'Perhaps we *should* listen, Art. I loved Lucy too, remember. I'm as sad as you are. And the professor tried very hard to save her life.'

So Holmwood listened as the professor patiently explained things to him.

'This is the worst thing that I have ever asked another man to do,' Van Helsing said. 'When Miss Lucy was alive, I was her friend, not just a doctor. I gave her my nights and my days. In my way, I loved her too. I will do anything to save her soul. This is the only way to do it. So that is why I must ask you to change your mind.'

Finally Arthur stood up, took Van Helsing's hand and said: 'It's hard – very hard. I can't really understand. But I'll go with you and wait.'

Some time after midnight the four men – Van Helsing, Dr Seward, Holmwood and Quincey Morris – stood in the Westenra family tomb. Van Helsing opened the top of Lucy's coffin, and told Holmwood and Morris to look inside.

There was a long silence. Then Arthur said in a low voice: 'Professor, I know that you are not playing a joke on me. You are too honest and serious for that. But somebody has stolen the body. This is a matter for the police.'

Van Helsing walked away without reply. When everybody was outside, he locked the door to the tomb. He took a white cloth from a bag that he had with him. Inside the cloth there was some bread. He took the bread, broke it into pieces, and pressed it into the space between the door and the stone wall of the tomb. He pressed more bread into the keyhole.

'This is holy bread,' he explained. 'I am closing the tomb and now nothing evil can get in.'

'What happens now?' Arthur asked. He was still unhappy about the disappearance of Lucy's body.

'Now,' said Van Helsing, 'prepare yourselves. You will need to be very brave. Let us wait behind this tree. We can watch the tomb from there.'

Nobody spoke. A soft wind blew through the trees, then died away. It left a deep, dreamlike silence. An hour passed, and then they saw something move. A white shape was passing through the trees.

The shape stepped out of the shadows into the moonlight, and everybody saw clearly. A golden-haired woman dressed in a white cloth was moving towards the tomb. She was holding a small child in her arms. It was Lucy – but a different Lucy. Her mouth was wet with the fresh blood of the child. It ran down her face. It coloured the white cloth that she was wearing.

Van Helsing stepped out. The woman stopped and, with an angry look, threw the child to the ground. Then she noticed Arthur, and moved towards him. Arthur moved back and hid his face in his hands, but she continued to walk towards him. Her face changed. She reached out her hand and said, in a sweet and lovely voice: 'Come to me, Arthur. Leave these others and come with me. My arms are hungry for you.'

Arthur took his hands away from his face and looked at her. He could not move. Her words of love danced in his head. She was beautiful, she was his Lucy . . .

Van Helsing was ready for this. Before Lucy could touch Arthur with her vampire's teeth, he jumped between them, a small gold cross in his hand. With a wild cry and the look of a hungry animal in her eyes, Lucy jumped back, then ran to the door of the tomb. But there again she stopped. She could not get in past the holy bread. Finally she ran into the shadow of a tree. The four men could see the white of her teeth shining in the darkness.

There was silence. At last Van Helsing, still holding up the cross, turned to Arthur. He asked: 'Now do I have your permission?'

Arthur went down on his knees and hid his face in his hands. 'Do what you have to do,' he said, and his voice was shaking. 'I've seen the worst already. Nothing can be as bad as that.'

As Dr Seward and Quincey ran to Arthur's side, the professor walked back to the door of the tomb. He pulled out some of the bread. Immediately, Lucy moved from the shadows and disappeared like smoke through the narrow space between the door and the wall of her tomb. Van Helsing then put the bread back.

'My friends,' he said, 'we can do nothing more before daylight. She cannot come out. She is tired, and she has not eaten for two nights. She will soon sleep. And then, we will do our work.'

◆

As the sky grew light, Van Helsing unlocked the door to the tomb again.

Lucy was asleep inside her coffin. She was more beautiful than ever. Arthur was much paler than she was. But he cried openly as he looked at her. Van Helsing did not have the same feelings. He could not see Lucy Westenra in the coffin. He could only see a vampire with the dried blood of a child around its mouth. He opened his bag and took out some doctor's knives and a thick, long, pointed piece of wood.

'Vampires cannot die of old age,' he said. 'They continue to live. They drink blood, and turn other people into vampires. She has already attacked those little children, but they will not suffer. But often people give their blood and then learn to love the vampire. They will become vampires after they die. There was a very great danger of that for you, my friend Arthur.

'But there is a way to save their souls. We can save them from a life of evil and an afterlife of endless punishment.' He pointed to the long, sharp piece of wood. 'It is a wonderful thing to save a soul. I can do it. But ...' he looked again at Arthur. 'But you should do it, because you loved her best.'

'Oh, my true friend,' said Arthur. 'Tell me what to do. I shan't fail.'

'Brave man,' said Van Helsing. 'Take this piece of wood in one hand and place the point over her heart. I shall read some words from this holy book, and then you must push the wood straight through the vampire's heart.'

Still pale, but with a strong hand, Arthur took the piece of wood and a heavy stone. Quincy Morris stood by his side. Van Helsing began to read, while Dr Seward placed the point exactly over the heart. Van Helsing finished reading. Arthur hit the wood with the stone as hard as he could.

The body in the coffin jumped, and the vampire's mouth produced a terrible scream. Its body turned this way and that

He could only see a vampire with the dried blood of a child around its mouth.

way, and its sharp teeth opened and shut. Its mouth was soon red with its own blood. But Arthur didn't stop. He hit the wood again and again, deeper and deeper into the vampire's heart. At last, it stopped fighting. There was no movement now.

'Before you leave this tomb,' Van Helsing said to Arthur, 'look for the last time at Lucy's face. She is not a vampire now. You have saved her soul.'

Arthur went down on his knees and kissed Lucy for the last time. Then he and Quincey walked, arm in arm, out into the sunlight.

Dr Seward and Van Helsing stayed in the tomb. They had to do one last job. They filled Lucy's mouth with garlic, and cut off her head. Then they shut the coffin for the last time. Outside, the professor gave the key of the tomb to Arthur.

'We have finished the first part of our work,' Van Helsing said. 'Now we must find and destroy the centre of this evil. I want to know: are you ready to follow me into even greater danger?'

One after the other, the three men shook Van Helsing's hand. They knew that he had to finish his terrible work. They promised to help him.

Chapter 9   Carfax House

Mina and Jonathan were married in Budapest, and they returned to England as man and wife. A few days after they arrived, they had a message from Arthur. Professor Van Helsing wanted to meet them.

Van Helsing met them at Paddington Station and took them back to his hotel. Mina told him about her holiday with Lucy in Whitby. Then Jonathan told his story.

'Why haven't you told anybody this story before now?' Van Helsing asked, when he finished. 'It is unbelievable.'

'Oh, Professor,' said Mina, looking at her husband's pale, lined face and greying hair. 'He's been very ill. It was weeks before he could even tell me the story.'

Van Helsing then told them everything that happened after Lucy's death. 'You will believe my story,' he said, 'as I believe yours. But no other people will believe us. So we are the only people who can fight this evil. And we can succeed with the information that you have both given me. I want you to join us. We are meeting tonight at Dr Seward's house. You, Mr Harker, know very well the dangers that I am asking you to join me in.'

◆

'. . . and so, my friends,' Van Helsing said, near the end of his little speech, 'these are the facts that we have discovered about our enemy. He is strong, but he also has weaknesses. He needs to rest during the hours of daylight, and this is his greatest weakness. If we can catch him in his box, we can destroy him.'

'But we need to know where these boxes are,' said Dr Seward.

'We do know,' replied Van Helsing, 'because Jonathan told us. They are not far from this room, in Carfax House!'

'Carfax House?' Jack Seward and Arthur Holmwood said together.

'Carfax is Dracula's house,' Jonathan explained. 'I know, because I helped him to buy it. I am sure that the boxes are there.'

'That explains why Renfield has been so excited,' said Seward. 'Two weeks ago he escaped and he ran to the doors of the old church next to Carfax House.'

'What are we waiting for?' cried Arthur. 'Let's go!'

'Not so fast,' said Van Helsing. 'We must first prepare ourselves.' He took a little, gold cross from his pocket, and a ring of garlic flowers from a box. He hung them both round Jonathan's neck. He did the same to Dr Seward, Arthur and Quincey. But when he came to Mina, he said: 'Madam Mina, I will not ask you to join us. It will not be a woman's work. You have already travelled far today and you will need to rest.'

Mina wanted to go with them, but Van Helsing refused.

◆

Jack Seward had a lot of old keys on a ring. He tried fourteen before the fifteenth turned. The door opened without a push. Van Helsing made a cross in the air with his right hand and went in first. The floor was dirty, and there was a terrible earthy smell.

'It's his breath,' said Jonathan. 'I remember it well.'

Van Helsing counted the earth-filled boxes that were piled against the walls. 'Twenty-nine,' he said angrily, turning to the others. 'That means that twenty-one boxes have already gone. The enemy is winning.' He started to count them again. Then he stopped when something touched his arm. It was Arthur's hand.

'What is the matter?' Van Helsing asked impatiently.

'I thought I saw a face,' Holmwood said, pointing towards one of the many dark passages around them. 'It was just for a second. A pale face with sharp, red eyes and an evil, smiling mouth.'

Nobody moved for a minute, and then Arthur put on a brave smile. 'It was probably just a shadow,' he said.

Quincey Morris walked towards the passage, holding a light high in his hand. 'There's no sign of anything,' he called back at last. 'Only walls.' But then he suddenly stepped back, and everybody jumped nervously. The old church seemed alive with movement. The shadowy corners and passages around them began to fill with a strange red light. Thousands of small, red stars began to shine out of the darkness.

'Rats!' Quincey shouted. 'Thousands of them!'

'Run for the doors!' Van Helsing cried, and everybody ran. There were rats everywhere – under their feet, in their hair, hanging on to their clothes . . .

At last they reached the door and shut it quickly. Outside, in the moonlight, it was safe. They took deep breaths of cold, fresh air.

'When we come back tomorrow,' Van Helsing said at last, 'Arthur must bring his dogs.'

'Tomorrow!' cried Dr Seward. 'I don't want to come back here ever again.'

'We have to,' was the reply. 'We must destroy these boxes. And then we must find the other twenty-one. Until we do that, we will never destroy the vampire.'

Chapter 10   Of One Blood

The five men were silent as they ate breakfast. Finally, Van Helsing spoke.

'Twenty-one boxes have gone,' he said, with a hopeless look in his eyes. 'He's probably taken them all over England.'

'That's a lot of boxes,' said Arthur. 'If they were taken out by day, perhaps someone at the hospital saw them. Carfax is very near, and they were probably taken out in the past three weeks.'

Dr Seward put his teacup down with a crash and hurried out of the room. He came back a minute later, waving a piece of paper at his surprised friends.

'Why didn't I think of this before?' he said excitedly. He told them the story of Renfield's attack on the men who were driving a cart along the road from Carfax House. 'I wrote down their names,' he said finally. 'Here they are, on this piece of paper. Thomas Snelling and Joseph Smollet. Renfield probably knew that they were taking Dracula away in one of the boxes.'

Van Helsing jumped to his feet. His tired eyes were alive again with new hope. 'Now we can make our plans!' he smiled.

One hour later, Jonathan was on his way to London to find

Smollet and Snelling. The other four returned to Carfax House.

By daylight the place was not as frightening. There were no rats, so Arthur's dogs were not needed. The professor opened every box and placed a piece of holy bread inside each one. 'No vampire will ever rest here again,' he said.

When the men returned, Mina was having breakfast. She looked a little pale and unwell. But she happily accepted Dr Seward's offer to show her round the hospital. She was very interested when the doctor told her about Renfield.

'Oh, please can I see him?' she said. 'He sounds very interesting.'

Seward was unhappy about this, but Mina had a very pretty smile. It was impossible to refuse her request.

Renfield was sitting quietly on his bed when Dr Seward brought Mina into his room.

'Good evening, Mr Renfield,' Mina said. 'Dr Seward has told me about you.'

Renfield made no immediate reply. He looked at her with a serious look on his face. Then, to Dr Seward's surprise, he said: 'You're not the girl that the doctor wanted to marry? No, that's impossible. She's dead.'

Mina smiled sweetly as she replied, 'Oh, no. I have a husband. I married him before I met Dr Seward. I'm Mrs Harker.'

'So what are you doing here?'

'My husband and I are visiting Dr Seward.'

'Don't stay.'

'Why not?'

Dr Seward thought that the conversation was becoming unpleasant for Mina. 'How did you know that I wanted to marry anyone?' he asked Renfield.

'That's a stupid question,' Renfield said, looking at Seward rudely. Then he turned again to Mina, smiled politely, and talked with her for many minutes about love and life. He even explained to Mina why he liked to eat living things. 'Blood is life, you know. Isn't that true, Doctor?'

Dr Seward was surprised at Renfield's soft voice and polite smile, so he agreed. Then, looking at his watch, he said: 'We must go now.'

'Goodbye, Mr Renfield,' Mina said. 'I hope we meet often. It's been very interesting.'

Renfield took her hand and looked into her eyes. 'Goodbye, my dear,' he said. 'I hope I never see your sweet face again.'

◆

At twenty minutes past midnight, Van Helsing was woken by a terrible cry. As he put on some clothes, he heard footsteps in the passage outside his door. It was the night guard, running towards Dr Seward's room with bad news. Renfield was hurt.

When the doctors reached Renfield's room, they found him on the floor. There was blood all over his face and head. He was alive, but his breaths were slow and difficult.

'Get your bag,' said Van Helsing. 'This is no simple accident. Something or somebody has tried to kill him. We must cut part of his head open immediately, or he will die. Perhaps he will be able to tell us what happened. That may help us.'

As Van Helsing shaved the hair off part of Renfield's broken head, Renfield's eyes opened. 'He came,' he said in a weak voice.

'Yes?' said Seward.

'He came to the window in a mist ... like last night. But last night he was a man, not a mist. He was outside the window, laughing at me. I didn't invite him in at first, but he promised me things. Living things that I could eat – rats, rats, rats – hundreds, thousands, millions of them, and dogs, and cats too ... All lives! All red blood, with years of life in it ... Without thinking, I opened the window. I invited him in. He came through the bars across my window, as thin as a piece of moonlight ... After that, I waited all day for him ...

'He came to the window in a mist. . .'

'Then Mrs Harker came to my room. I could see from her pale face that he visited her last night. He wanted to visit her again tonight. I was angry with him when I thought of Mrs Harker. She was nice and kind to me. I didn't want him to take the life from her, so tonight I was ready for him.

'When I saw the green mist coming into my room, I held it tight. I know I'm a madman. And madmen are unnaturally strong. I fought him. I was winning – until I saw his eyes . . . They burned into me like fire. I couldn't hold him. A great weakness came over me and then . . .' Renfield's voice became quieter and quieter. Then he was silent. Dr Seward took his hand. He was dead.

Without a word, Van Helsing and Seward ran upstairs. They met Arthur and Quincey in the passage outside Mina's room. They stopped and listened at the door.

'Everything seems quiet,' Seward said softly. 'Can we believe the words of a madman?'

'We must check,' said Van Helsing. He tried the door, but it was locked. Arthur threw himself at the door, and it fell open. The four men stood in the doorway. They couldn't believe what they saw.

Moonlight shone through the open window, filling the room with silver light and throwing large, black shadows across the walls. Mina was on her knees at the foot of her bed in her white nightdress. By her side stood a tall, thin man dressed in black. The front of his shirt was open. His left hand held both of Mina's hands tightly. His right hand was on the back of Mina's neck, pressing her face against his chest. At first, they looked like lovers. But there was blood on Mina's nightdress, and blood ran from a wound in the man's neck to his chest. He was pushing her mouth into the blood.

The man turned his face to the four men in the doorway. His eyes burned red. He opened his mouth, and showed his terrible, sharp, white teeth. Then he threw Mina away from him on to the bed and prepared to jump.

At first, they looked like lovers.

Van Helsing realized what was happening. He held his cross out towards the vampire. Dr Seward, Arthur and Quincey did the same. The vampire screamed, and a mist filled the room. When the mist cleared a few minutes later, the vampire, Count Dracula, wasn't there.

'It was like a dream,' Mina said weakly from the bed a few minutes later. 'The same dream as the night before. I was falling asleep, when a man with shining eyes came to my bed. He opened his shirt and, with his own fingernails, pulled open his neck and pressed my mouth to his blood. While I drank, he said: "Now we have one blood and one mind. You have helped my enemies, but soon you will help me."'

There was silence after she spoke.

'But is it true, professor?' she continued, with tears in her eyes, taking his hand. 'Am I tied to him for ever? When I die, must I become...?'

'My child,' replied Van Helsing, looking suddenly old and grey. 'You are with friends. We will give our lives to keep you safe. We have been careless, but we will not be careless again. The vampire thinks that he has won tonight. But he is wrong.'

Chapter 11   A Race Against Time

Jonathan almost lost his mind when he heard the news about Mina. He hit his head with his hands and cried wildly, like a madman. 'Dracula. It's Dracula ... and it's all because of me ...!'

But Mina and Van Helsing calmed him, and soon he was able to talk about his visit to London. 'I know where the other boxes are,' he said. 'I paid Smollet and Snelling, and I have the address.'

'Then we must go there quickly,' Van Helsing said. 'But first we must find a way to guard Mina.'

'I'm coming with you,' Mina said. 'You'll see – I won't be afraid.'

At the London address, the five men and Mina found all except one of Dracula's boxes. They destroyed them, but they did not find the count.

That night they guarded Mina carefully. In the morning Dr Seward asked her how she felt.

'A little tired,' she said. 'I was dreaming so much. In my dreams I was always on a boat, and I could hear water.'

Dr Seward turned to the professor. 'Perhaps she can read Dracula's mind while she's asleep?'

'Perhaps,' Van Helsing agreed. 'If she can, Dracula is leaving the country by sea inside his last box. He is going home. But which ship is the box on?'

'Why do we want to know?' Mina asked. 'He's leaving the country. Isn't that enough?'

Van Helsing took her hands. 'Madam Mina, that was true a week ago, before you drank the vampire's blood. But now we have to save your soul. We must destroy him.'

◆

They discovered that one ship, the *Tsarina Catherine*, sailed that morning from London for the Black Sea. The ship's office said that, at the last minute, a man put a box on the ship. He paid a lot of money.

The five men and Mina immediately caught a train to Paris. From there they took a fast train to Varna, and waited for the *Tsarina Catherine*. They waited for almost two weeks with no news of the ship. Every night Mina dreamed of a boat and the sound of water. Every day Van Helsing and Dr Seward watched her for signs of change. They checked her teeth, her eyes, her skin.

Two weeks after they arrived in Varna, there was a thick sea

45

mist. No one saw the *Tsarina Catherine* when it sailed past the port and up the River Danube to Galatz, 185 miles nearer Castle Dracula than Varna.

'He knows that we are waiting for him,' Van Helsing said. 'Madam Mina can read his mind, but we are forgetting. He can probably read her mind, too.'

They caught a train to Galatz. There, they found a man who knew about the box. They had to make new plans. After a long discussion, everybody agreed that Dracula was probably going back to his castle by river.

'I think that the best plan of action for us will be this,' Van Helsing said. 'Arthur and Jonathan will take a boat and go after the vampire up the river. Jack and Quincey, I want you to follow the river on horseback. Mina and I will take the train to Veresti and from there we will go towards the castle.'

Before they went their different ways, Van Helsing spoke quietly to Seward. 'Have you noticed, Jack? Madam Mina is changing. I can see the vampire coming into her face. Some of her teeth are sharper. At times her soft eyes become unusually hard. That is why I want her husband to go with Arthur. He must not see these changes in her. I will stay with Madam Mina. I know how to protect her. Now go. Every hour is very important. We cannot fail.'

◆

Jonathan and Arthur spent two days on the river. They sailed by day and by night, but they passed only a few boats and these were too small for a large, heavy box. But on the third day, they passed into the Bistritza. There they heard from some passing Slovaks that there was a big boat on the river in front of them. It was going unusually fast. Jonathan and Arthur were filled with hope.

But the river became narrow and rocky and bad luck hit them. They had an accident, and they had to stop and mend the boat. They lost many hours, and also the weather was getting worse. They were now only about thirty-five miles from Bistritz, so they decided to leave the boat at the next small town. They rode from there on horseback by small country roads towards their meeting place with Mina and the professor.

◆

The professor and Mina arrived at Veresti at midday on the last day of October. The professor found a carriage that could take them sixty-two miles from Veresti through the mountains along the Bistritz road. He also bought food and warmer clothes.

'Perhaps we will not see a town again for a week,' he explained.

The roads were bad, but Van Helsing never got tired. He drove with only the shortest stops for sleep. Every time he reached a village, he changed horses. They reached the Bistritz road on the second day. Mina slept, but she stopped dreaming of water. So Dracula was now travelling by land towards his castle. Then, as they climbed higher into the mountains, Mina seemed to take a greater interest in the road.

Two hours later, through the trees, they saw a dark shape in the clouds, high above them. It was the mountain-top home of the vampire – Castle Dracula.

Van Helsing drove off the road and stopped under some trees. Snow was in the air, so he made a fire. While Mina sat quietly by the fire, Van Helsing drew a circle in the ground around her with a stick. He dropped small pieces of holy bread inside the circle. Then he waited outside the circle and watched Mina.

'Mina,' he called. 'Come here.'

Without answering, Mina got up. She began to walk towards him, but suddenly she stopped. She seemed unable to take another step. Van Helsing reached out his hand to her.

'Come,' he repeated.

She shook her head and went down on her knees. He was right. She was already half-vampire, and she could not leave the circle. But if she could not leave it, others could not go in. 'I shall be safe inside the circle,' he thought. 'And Mina will be safe too. I only hope that I shall be safe from Mina.'

Darkness came. Sometimes the horses made frightened noises. Van Helsing went to them and calmed them. He was tired. But he was afraid to sleep while Mina was awake.

At about three o'clock in the morning, the fire began to die down. They needed some wood before the snow got worse. Van Helsing stood up, but Mina stopped him. 'Don't leave the circle now. Stay where you're safe.'

'I am worried about *you*,' he replied.

Mina gave a strange, deep laugh. 'Don't worry about me. Nobody's safer from them than I am.'

Van Helsing did not understand, but then the horses screamed again. He looked and saw, in the darkness, three women outside the circle. They were beautiful, and they moved in a slow, strange dance. 'These are the women who drank Jonathan's blood,' he thought. They reached out their arms, calling for Mina. He could feel Mina's growing excitement.

He was afraid that the circle was not strong enough to protect him. He picked up a piece of burning wood and threw it at the women. They screamed, and disappeared.

Silence returned. He felt more tired than ever. He wanted to sleep, but Mina was looking at him in a strange way. He was sure now. It was not safe to sleep in her company. She was now almost a vampire.

◆

Day came slowly. It stopped snowing, but the skies were still heavy and grey. Jonathan, Dr Seward, Arthur and Quincey rode as fast as they could. They were not far behind their enemy. On the mountain road above them, they saw a cart and a number of men on horseback. They rode without stopping all day, but the cart with Dracula in his box was moving too fast. It was a race against time.

Suddenly they heard a gunshot. Jonathan pulled out his Indian knife. Quincey put his hand on his gun. They were filled with a nervous excitement. The end was near.

The men were standing around the cart with knives in their hands. Van Helsing stood in the middle of the road in front of them, holding a gun. They seemed unsure of their next step. He was one and they were many. He had a gun, but they could all attack at the same time ...

Suddenly, four horsemen rode straight at them. Jonathan was riding the fastest. He waved his knife and screamed like a madman. The men were too surprised to act. Jonathan and Quincey jumped off their horses and ran to the cart. There was a short fight. Quincey fell to the ground, holding his side. Minutes later, most of the men were running away down the mountainside. It was almost dark. They had to reach Dracula before the light disappeared.

While Arthur, Van Helsing and Dr Seward fought the last of Dracula's helpers, Jonathan jumped on to the cart. Quincey, in great pain, climbed up with him. The body inside was beginning to move. Dracula's eyes were opening. His mouth was forming an evil smile.

They didn't have a sharp piece of wood, so Jonathan pushed his knife down hard into Dracula's neck. Quincey pushed a knife straight into Dracula's heart. Dracula opened his mouth and produced a long, terrible scream. Again and again the men cut into his neck and heart with their knives until Dracula's head came away from his body. For a second Dracula's face continued to scream, then suddenly there was silence. They watched, unable to look away. A quiet look of restful sleep came over the vampire's face, and his body disappeared. Seconds later, they were looking into an empty box.

Mina saw that Quincey was hurt. She ran out of the holy circle towards him. He was lying on his back, and blood from the wound in his side was falling into the snow. As Jonathan held Quincey's head, Mina took his hand and said: 'We've won. We've beaten him.'

Quincey took a deep breath and looked up at Mina. 'I'm glad I could help,' he said. Then, with a smile, the American adventurer closed his eyes and died.

Mina stood up slowly. She was very sad at the death of a brave, dear friend. Jonathan took her in his arms and kissed her. Arthur sat by Quincey's body, with a lost look in his eyes. Van Helsing looked at Seward.

'Have you noticed it too?' he said.

Seward knew what the professor meant. Mina's face was different now. The long teeth, the unnatural colour of her skin, the strange look in her eye – they were not there now. She was the real Mina again. Her soul was saved.

ACTIVITIES

Chapters 1–3

Before you read

1 Write down five things that you know about *Dracula* from books or films. Compare your list with another student. Have you written the same things?

2 Find these words in your dictionary. They are all in the story.

breath carriage cart castle evil mad mist passage servant wolf

Which are words for:

a a home?   **c** an animal?

b vehicles?   **d** a person?

Which word describes:

e a place between rooms?

f air that goes in and out of your body?

g a thin cloud?

h a sick person?

i something that is very, very bad?

After you read

3 Choose the correct answer.

a At first Jonathan thinks that Dracula is:

(i) ugly.

(ii) evil.

(iii) unusual.

b When Jonathan sees the three women, he:

(i) tries to run away.

(ii) wants them to touch him.

(iii) hopes for their help.

c Jonathan doesn't kill Dracula because:

(i) something mysterious stops him.

(ii) he's too frightened.

(iii) he can't move.

d When Dracula leaves the castle, Jonathan feels:

    (i) lonely.

    (ii) angry.

    (iii) unsafe.

4 What is unusual about Dracula and

    a food? **b** servants? **c** mirrors? **d** his face and hands?

5 How are these important to the story?

    a a cross **b** a key **c** letters

Chapters 4–8

Before you read

6 How will Mina feel when she gets Jonathan's letters from Castle Dracula? Why?

7 Find these words in your dictionary. Put them in the sentences.

    bat coffin garlic professor soul tomb vampire wound

    a He died abroad from a terrible ..... . His body was brought back in a ..... . It was then placed in the family ..... .

    b A ..... is a small animal that flies at night. A ..... also moves at night, but it is more dangerous!

    c She is a ..... of religious studies at the university, and her special interest is the nature of the ..... .

    d Have you eaten ..... today?

8 Find the word *holy* in your dictionary. Which of these things can be *holy*, and why?

    a man a city a dog a book a gun bread

After you read

9 Who are these sentences about?

    a She loves him best.   **e** He drinks his blood.

    b He is angry with him.   **f** He gives her blood.

    c He tells him to listen.   **g** He cuts her head off.

    d He believes him first.   **h** They are away when she dies.

10 After Van Helsing's visit, how many times is Lucy unprotected from the vampire? Why?

11 How are these important in the fight to save Lucy's soul?

    a holy bread **b** garlic **c** a piece of wood **d** knives

Chapters 9–11

Before you read

12 Who is in the greatest danger from Dracula now? Why?

13 Find the word *rat* in your dictionary. Do you like *rats*? Why (not)?

After you read

14 How do Renfield's feelings about Dracula change? Why?

15 Work with another student. Act out this conversation.

Student A: You are Mina. Tell Jonathan why you want to go to Transylvania.

Student B: You are Jonathan. You don't want Mina to go to Transylvania with you. Tell her why.

16 In this story, how many different things does Dracula change himself into?

Writing

17 You are Jonathan. Write a letter to Mina from Dracula's Castle. Tell her what has *really* happened to you. Ask her for help.

18 You are Dr Seward. Write a report about Lucy's illness, from the first time you visited her to her death.

19 You are Van Helsing. Write something for a medical magazine. Answer the question: What Do You Do When A Vampire Attacks?

20 Write a police description of Dracula, with the title:

WANTED FOR MURDER

Tell people not to go near him. Say why.